Memori

Andrew Devonshire

By Deborah Devonshire

Published by

Ashbourne Hall, Cokayne Ave
Ashbourne, Derbyshire, DE6 1EJ England
Tel: (01335) 347349 Fax: (01335) 347303
e-mail: landmark@clara.net

1st Edition

13 ISBN: 978-1-84306-366-7

10 ISBN: 1-84306-366-2

CS

British Library Cataloguing in Publication Data: a catalogue record for this book is available from the British Library.

Print: Gutenberg Press, Malta

Design by: Sarah Labuhn

Front Cover: Detail from 'Andrew Cavendish, 11th Duke of Devonshire, 1992-93' by Stephen Conroy.

Back Cover: Andrew and Deborah in the Flower Room at Chatsworth.

Memories of
Andrew Devonshire

By Deborah Devonshire

Landmark Publishing

Acknowledgements

Two American friends went round the exhibition at Chatsworth devoted to Andrew's life and said "Why don't you make it into a book?" So this volume is thanks to them.

Most of the photographs are securely fixed into our family albums, so it has not always been possible to identify the photographers for which I offer my apologies.

I am extremely grateful for the generosity of the following in giving permission to use their work:-
Bill Burlington, Stephen Conroy, Peter Drew, Ron Duggins, Bridget Flemming, Ian Fraser-Martin, Gary Rogers, Keith Stynes, Christopher Simon Sykes, Simon Upton and Eva Zielinska-Millar. Special thanks to the Buxton Museum & Art Gallery for the Boards of Buxton photographs.

I would like to thank my old friend Lucian Freud for allowing me to reproduce his work.

The photograph on page 47 is courtesy of the Norman Parkinson Archive; on page 66 (bottom) by permission of Elizabeth Banks; and on page 83 by permission of David Hastings.

I also wish to thank Diane Naylor, Photo Librarian at Chatsworth, Lindsey Porter of Landmark Publishing Ltd for his enthusiasm in the publication of this book, and Sarah Labuhn and Michelle Hunt, designers, for putting it all together in double-quick time.

There would be no book without Helen Marchant, who was Andrew's secretary for 17 years. She was instrumental in arranging the exhibition and has done an immense amount of work in preparing this publication. My grateful thanks are to her.

Deborah Devonshire.
August 2007.

FAMILY TREE

VICTOR, 9th Duke
1868-1938
m. Lady Evelyn Fitzmaurice
1870-1960

EDWARD, 10th Duke
1895-1950
m. Lady Mary Cecil
1895-1988

Maud
1896-1975
m1. Capt Angus Mackintosh
1 daughter
m2. Brig Hon George Baillie
2 sons, 1 daughter

Blanche
1898-1987
m. Lt Col Ivan Cobbold
2 sons, 2 daughters

Dorothy
1900-1966
m. Harold Macmillan
later 1st Earl of Stockton
1 son, 3 daughters

Rachel
1902-77
m. James Stuart
later Viscount Stuart of Findhorn
2 sons

Charles
1905-44
m. Adele Astaire

Anne
1909-81
m1. Henry Hunloke
2 sons, 1 daughter
m2. Christopher Holland-Martin
m3. Alexander Montagu

William
1917-44
m. Kathleen Kennedy

ANDREW, 11th Duke
1920-2004
m. Hon. Deborah Mitford
b. 1920

Elizabeth
b. 1926

Anne
b. 1927
m. Michael Tree
2 daughters

Emma
b. 1943
m. Hon Tobias Tennant

PEREGRINE, 12th Duke
b. 1944
m. Amanda Heywood-Lonsdale

Sophia
b. 1957
m1. Anthony Murphy   m2. Alastair Morrison   m3. Will Topley

Edward
b. 1967
m. Emma Bridgeman

Stella
b. 1970
m. David Lasnet

Isabel
b. 1964
m. Piers Hill

WILLIAM
Earl of Burlington
b.1969
m. Laura née Roundell

Celina
b. 1971
m. Alexander Carter

Jasmine
b. 1973
m. Nicholas Dunne

Declan
b. 1993

Nancy
b. 1995

Contents

'Andrew Cavendish, 11th Duke of Devonshire, 1992-93' by Stephen Conroy

— Early Years —

Andrew Robert Buxton Cavendish was born on 2nd January 1920. The name Buxton was added because his father was Mayor of the Borough that year.

His childhood and education were conventional. Unusually, he liked his private school better than Eton. He was brought up in a household where politics was the inherited interest. His father followed his family's traditional path to the House of Commons, representing West Derbyshire till he became Duke of Devonshire and had to move to the House of Lords in 1938. His mother was Mary Cecil whose grandfather, Lord Salisbury, was Prime Minister three times between 1885–1902.

Andrew & his elder brother William (Billy) with their parents at Chatsworth, 1923

Andrew & Billy as pages at the wedding of
their aunt Rachel Cavendish and James Stuart,
August 1923

Billy & Andrew, c.1926

Billy was two years older than Andrew. The arrival of Elizabeth in 1926 and Anne in 1927 completed the family. They lived at Churchdale Hall, Ashford-in-the-Water, five miles from Chatsworth and later on at Compton Place in Eastbourne. When the House of Commons was sitting they lived in London.

Right:
Andrew (far right) with his brother, mother and sisters

Below:
Churchdale Hall, Ashford-in-the-Water, Derbyshire

Andrew dressed as a page for a performance at
Madame Vacani's dancing school, 1927

Andrew, c. 1928

Above:
Billy & Andrew with
the High Peak Harriers

Right:
Eton schoolboys
– Andrew & his cousin
Richard Cavendish

The boys were taught by a French governess till they went to Ludgrove preparatory school.

In 1933 Andrew went to Eton College. He described himself there as "dirty, lazy, and always on the borderline in trials [examinations]."

Victor, 9th Duke of Devonshire, with 16 of his 21 grandchildren, Christmas 1931.
Andrew is third from right

Billy, Andrew, Anne & Elizabeth with their father at Bolton Abbey, Yorkshire, c. 1938

A university point-to-point at Cottenham, near Cambridge, c.1940

Andrew with his father and dogs, Studley, Benjy & Bootle, at Compton Place, July 1943. Andrew was on leave just before embarking for Italy with the Coldstream Guards

Marriage

Andrew and I met at a dinner party before a dance in London in April 1938 when we were both eighteen.

Andrew

Deborah Mitford,
youngest daughter of 2nd Baron Redesdale

Andrew & Deborah

We were married at St Bartholomew the Great, London, on 19th April 1941 during the Blitz.

My father, in Home Guard
uniform, gave me away

Elizabeth & Anne
with their parents

Above: Being congratulated by
Regimental Sergeant Major Brittain

Left: 19th April 1941 – we were both just 21

Below: Second Lieutenant Lord and
Lady Andrew Cavendish

The reception was held at 26 Rutland Gate, my father's London house. The windows had been blown out during a raid two nights before and wallpaper made improvised curtains.

Cutting the cake

Lady Redesdale, the Duke of Devonshire, myself, Lord Redesdale, Andrew, Billy Hartington and the Duchess of Devonshire

Leaving the wedding reception at Rutland Gate

Our few days' honeymoon were spent at Compton Place, the Devonshire's home at Eastbourne. We heard the drone of German bombers flying overhead towards London and back again every night.

Military Service

When war broke out in 1939 Andrew was at Cambridge University and was called up the following year. He went to the Brigade of Guards Depot at Caterham and then to Sandhurst to join the Coldstream Guards, in which his brother was already serving. Discipline was harsh – luckily some of the other embryo officers were old friends who helped each other through the severity of initiation into army life.

At the Guards Depot, Caterham,
spring 1940

2nd Lieutenant, Coldstream Guards,
autumn 1940

With Emma and Peregrine & dogs at The Rookery, Ashford-in-the-Water, 1945

Two and a half years of training and frustrating inactivity were to come. Then in 1943 Andrew's battalion embarked for Italy to reinforce the regiment whose numbers were severely depleted in the North African campaign and subsequently at Salerno. They experienced some fierce fighting as they advanced to Rome and on north to Florence.

During a lull in combat Andrew's fellow Coldstreamer and our old friend, Tom Egerton, got the news that on 27th April 1944 the baby I was expecting had been born – a boy – a cheering message for Andrew at that moment.

When Andrew was still in England I followed the drum when it was practical to do so, before setting up house at The Rookery, Ashford-in-the-Water, on the Chatsworth estate in 1946. By this time I had two babies, Emma (b.1943) and Peregrine (b.1944), having lost the first who sadly was born prematurely and did not survive.

This photograph was used in Andrew's political election campaign, 1945.

He left the army with the rank of Captain.

Andrew won a Military Cross for gallantry during the advance, describing the event as "having some anxious moments...", every mile being hotly contested by the enemy. He seldom talked of the searing experiences of war as a 24-year-old temporary major, but when he did it was of the camaraderie and his admiration of the non-commissioned officers and the men. Years later, he sometimes said he wished he had stayed in the army

General Poole awarding the Military Cross for gallantry, 1944

Lord Granby, Lady Irene Haig, Andrew, Billy and Hugo Waterhouse
at Billy's coming of age celebrations at Chatsworth, 1939

Billy's marriage to Kathleen Kennedy, May 1944, with Billy's parents and Joe Kennedy Jr

Then came the tragic event which changed Andrew's future. On 9th September 1944 Billy Hartington was killed by a sniper's bullet in Belgium. Andrew was deeply shocked by his brother's death. Not only had he lost his old companion but he had to face the fact that he himself was now his father's heir.

Billy & Andrew, c. 1942

With Emma and Peregrine after moving to Edensor House in 1946

Inheritance

Andrew was brought up very much as the second son, one who would expect little or nothing of the considerable fortune owned by his father. His plans for a job after the war were hardly formulated but his love of books inclined him to think of a career in publishing. Politics also loomed large, a family tradition from which few Cavendishes had deviated.

In the autumn of 1950 Andrew went to Australia at his father's request. The Duke wished to invest there and Andrew was to explore the possibilities. His stay was cut short by the sudden and unexpected death of the Duke on November 26th. He was 55 years old. Andrew lost his father, friend and counsellor, and once again our lives were turned upside down with the huge responsibilities which he now had to face.

Chatsworth

Lismore Castle, Co. Waterford

In his autobiography "*Accidents of Fortune*" Andrew describes the burden of death duties at 80% on everything his father owned. All the family assets were depleted by that amount – land, works of art, stocks & shares. It took seventeen years to pay the enormous bill with interest accruing at £1,000 a day.

With little public sympathy for his plight, Andrew set about the painful decisions on what he must sell and how a viable future could be provided for his family and his employees from the remaining assets.

Bolton Hall, Bolton Abbey, North Yorkshire

Compton Place, Eastbourne

Chatsworth

Andrew also found himself responsible for hundreds of employees and their families

Above: A celebration for staff who had completed 25 years or more service, 1963. 52 had worked at Chatsworth for over 40 years

This sorry state of affairs occupied Andrew and his lawyers for two decades. Chatsworth was always at the centre of their deliberations, to keep it in the family was the seemingly hopeless aim. One of Andrew's decisions, which he never regretted, was taken in 1954. He offered Hardwick Hall, its incomparable contents and 3,000 acres of surrounding farmland to the Treasury in lieu of cash owed on it. The offer was accepted and the government handed it over to The National Trust. Andrew was grateful to the Trust for the wonderful way they have restored both Bess's fantastic house and its equally remarkable tapestries and embroideries.

Hardwick Hall, c. 1955

Sales reduced the land ownership from 120,000 acres to about 67,000 acres. Some of the most important works of art were taken by the government in lieu of cash and were transferred by them to national museums.

However, this enforced streamlining strengthened Chatsworth's central position in the management of what remained.

The visit of HRH The Princess Elizabeth and The Duke of Edinburgh, Edensor House, 1948

In the garden at Edensor House, c. 1950

Outside our London house on Coronation day, 1953

In our robes for the Coronation, 1953. Peregrine was page to my mother-in-law who was Mistress of the Robes to Her Majesty The Queen. He had special permission to perform this duty as he was only 9 and the approved age was 12

Eventually the future became clearer. Andrew and his land agent decided it would be desirable for Chatsworth for us to move back into the house, which had been vacated by his parents in 1939 when Penrhos College, a girls' school of 300 pupils and staff, made it their war-time home. I have described this big undertaking in my book "*Chatsworth – The House*".

The Library at Chatsworth after Penrhos College left in 1946,
showing the muddle of treasures hastily stored

The Great Dining Room as a wartime dormitory

Above: In the garden, with south and east fronts of Chatsworth behind,
after the catastrophic gale in January 1962.

Below: Aerial photograph of Chatsworth, c. 1952

Politics

When Andrew came home from Italy he was determined to stand as a Conservative candidate in the 1945 election – Billy having unsuccessfully fought a bitter by-election for West Derbyshire, in 1944, then rejoining his regiment only to die for those whom he had wished to serve in Parliament.

Andrew was turned down for Mile End and another East End of London constituency – not a propitious start. Undeterred he tried elsewhere and was eventually chosen to fight the Conservative cause in Chesterfield. This is the nearest big town to Chatsworth and was then a centre of heavy industry and surrounded by coal mines. The campaign was an education for both of us, bringing us into contact with people we would never have met otherwise. There were three or four meetings every night for three weeks. Andrew became a brilliant speaker and adept at answering questions, and he made his audience laugh, often against loud heckling. It became quite rough at times, we were spat at, the crowd tried to turn over our car, and once Andrew was tripped up and fell heavily while hurrying to answer a call to shake the hand of a Staveley miner.

Addressing the crowd in Chesterfield Market Place, 1945

Right: Manifesto for the General Election campaign, 1950

Below: Electioneering in the 1945 campaign

In spite of a wonderful band of enthusiastic helpers, he was never going to win Chesterfield but he made many friends and stayed on to nurse the constituency for the next election. After becoming duke in 1950, Andrew had to proceed to the House of Lords and made his maiden speech during the Suez Crisis of 1956.

Electioneering with his sister Anne, 1945

Andrew congratulating the victor George Benson in the General Election campaign of 1945, with Mr Clegg, Town Clerk

Ministerial Office

Perhaps the happiest time for Andrew was when he was a member of his Uncle Harold (Macmillan)'s government (1960-64). Politics was always in his mind and, although by this time he was deeply committed to life in Derbyshire and looking after his other estates, as well as working for many charities and acting as a Steward of the Jockey Club, Uncle Harold's offer of Parliamentary Under-Secretary of State in the Commonwealth Relations Office was not resisted. The job suited him perfectly. It involved a lot of travel to the freedom ceremonies of many former colonies during the final break-up of the Empire. Andrew's good manners and easy ways made him popular with his hosts and any references to nepotism regarding his appointment were soon forgotten.

Official photograph as Minister of State for Commonwealth Relations, 1960

Myself, Sophia, Emma, Harold Macmillan, Andrew, Mary Devonshire & Peregrine at Chatsworth

Hugh Fraser MP, Andrew, Harold Macmillan, Lord Arran & myself on Bolton moor, Yorkshire

Two of the independence ceremonies were memorable. On the final night of British rule in Kenya there was a ball. Andrew danced with four of Kenyatta's wives, three black and one white, and all seemed to enjoy themselves immensely. At the similar event in Kingston, Jamaica, Vice-President Johnson represented the United States. He was not a popular figure. Andrew offered £10 to whoever of our party was the first to dance with him. Without hesitation Antonia Fraser (Hugh Fraser MP was a British government representative) cut in, was whirled round the floor and claimed the reward.

Outside the Oba's palace, Lagos, September 1961

With the Oba of Lagos, the Olota of Otta and Lady Dorothea Head, wife of the British High Commissioner, September 1961

Meeting Nigerian journalists, July 1963

With Dr Nnamdi Azikiwe, first President of Nigeria, 1963

My one regret for Andrew was that he only had one boss (Duncan Sandys) during his four years of government service. It narrowed the experience. Nevertheless those years made up a little for having failed to become an MP as a younger man.

In the 1980s Andrew decided to join the Social Democratic Party. In the final days of hereditary peers he sat on the cross-benches in the House of Lords.

With the Ugandan Minister of Information outside the House of Commons, April 1963

Top: The Shah of Persia's visit to Chatsworth, 1964

Above Left: The Sardauna of Sokoto admiring the painting of Henry VIII after Holbein in the Library at Chatsworth. He was murdered in January 1965

Above Right: The President of India stayed at Chatsworth, June 1963

In 1964 Harold Macmillan's successor, Alec Douglas-Home, rewarded Andrew by appointing him a Privy Counsellor.

The Kennedy Family

The Kennedys played an important part in the lives of the Cavendish family from the day they arrived with Joseph P. as US Ambassador to London in 1938. Joe Junior, Jack, Eunice and Kick (Kathleen) were very much part of the London scene in 1938 and '39. Andrew's brother, Billy Hartington, married Kick in May 1944, after opposition on religious grounds from both sides were settled. Three months later he was killed in action.

So when Jack became President of the United States in 1961 we were invited to his Inauguration and were welcomed as family, travelling to and from the various ceremonies and festivities in the bus with 'Kennedy Family' emblazoned on the front. It was the first of several visits to The White House which Andrew records in his book. Andrew's first cousin, David Ormsby-Gore, later Lord Harlech, was a great friend of JFK and his appointment by Uncle Harold as Ambassador to Washington made the "special relationship" with Britain special indeed.

We were in Washington during the Cuban missile crisis. Andrew was amazed by an apparently relaxed President finding time to talk to him for half an hour in The Oval Office and walking with him in the garden at such an anxious time.

President Kennedy's visit to his sister's grave at Edensor, 29 June 1963

Bobby and
Ethel Kennedy's
visit to Edensor,
January 1964

Teddy and Joan
Kennedy at
Edensor, May
1965

The President came to Chatsworth in June 1963 to visit the grave of his beloved sister Kick. Her tragic death in a plane crash in 1948 affected her brother deeply. She was his acknowledged favourite in the family.

We both went to the funeral of the assassinated President, which Andrew describes so well in his book. He also attended Bobby Kennedy's funeral in 1968 and reflected on the resilience through her unshakeable Catholic faith of their mother, Rose Kennedy, in the face of such terrible losses.

Family Life

At Bakewell Show, August 1946. Lady Anne Holland-Martin & Ellen Stephens ('Diddy' the children's beloved nanny) are left and right of myself and Andrew

With HRH The Princess Margaret at Royal Ascot, 1950

The family in the Blue Drawing Room at Chatsworth
photographed by Norman Parkinson for Vogue, 1952

Sophia's christening, 1957

In 1947 & 1953 two more babies were born but did not survive, so the safe arrival of Sophia in 1957 was the greatest joy to us both.

At a Royal Academy dinner, c. 1965.

We were lucky to lead unusual lives and have the chance to meet so many people who later became well-known in politics, agriculture, gardening, literature and the stage. The background of Chatsworth, Bolton Abbey, Lismore and Compton Place enabled us to have friends to stay, to travel, to go racing and generally to enjoy ourselves, as well as paying attention to the more serious side of life. Later on our children invited their friends and we all appreciated the efforts of the staff who made it all possible.

—— Public Life ——

Andrew's life gradually moved into the pattern it followed for the next 44 years. Public service came first for him and charitable work of all kinds ruled. He had already been Mayor of Buxton for two years (1952-54). Buxton was closely connected with the Cavendish family since Bess of Hardwick's last husband, Lord Shrewsbury, was custodian of Mary, Queen of Scots, who regularly took the waters there.

In the 1780s the 5th Duke of Devonshire engaged Carr of York to build the beautiful Crescent and stables there. The latter became the Devonshire Royal Hospital and, much to Andrew's delight, is now playing a vital role as part of the University of Derby.

Above:
Mayor &
Mayoress of
Buxton,
1952-54

Left:
Mayor-making
procession,
Buxton 1952

Above: 7th World Congress of the International Society for the Welfare of Cripples, 1957

Andrew was tireless in his efforts for the charities he supported – giving generously himself, writing thousands of letters, leading major fundraising campaigns and hosting gala events. He used his honorary positions to good effect, bringing together interested and influential people in convivial surroundings at Chatsworth or in London, to the benefit of all.

He enjoyed meeting those involved – he liked nothing better than a cup of tea and a chat with people in hospital, the old, the young or disabled, and his admiration for their carers was unceasing. In this way he made many good friends who often found themselves being persuaded to join another cause he was championing.

Some of the "entertainments" to which he willingly went were excruciatingly long and dull, but he always found something or somebody who got his attention and made it worthwhile.

Below: Her Majesty The Queen Mother visiting the Royal Hospital & Home for Incurables, Putney, of which Andrew was President for many years

Addressing the 7th World Congress of the International Society for the Welfare of Cripples, 1957

Andrew was Chancellor of the University of Manchester for 21 years from 1965.
In 2002 he was awarded the Freedom of the Borough of Eastbourne.

Above: Preparing for a degree awards ceremony at the University of Manchester

Right: Greeting Her Majesty The Queen on a visit to the University of Manchester

Presentation of new colours to the 1st Battalion, Sherwood Foresters Regiment, May 1965

BARNARDO
HOUSE

Above: Outside Barnardo House, London with Regional Organiser David Brown

Right: Greeting Her Majesty The Queen at the Royal première of the film 'Dr Doolittle' in December 1967, on behalf of an African medical charity

Opposite page:

Top: Derby County Football Club's Championship winning team visiting Chatsworth c. 1972

Bottom: Hosting a visit from members of the Royal Smithfield Club, July 1975, with myself as President

Andrew c. 1985

Above & Right:
8,000 volunteers
and supporters
attended the
Barnardo's garden
party on the
Salisbury Lawns at
Chatsworth, 4 July
1986. HRH The
Princess of Wales
spent the day with
them and later
planted a tree in
the west garden

Above:
At the time of his death Andrew had over 300 ties representing societies, clubs and organisations with which he was associated

Right:
Mary Robinson, President of Ireland, planting a tree on her visit to Lismore Castle, 1993

Opposite Page:

Top:
Andrew with Dame Norma Major and representatives of the MENCAP Blue Sky Appeal, February 1997

Bottom:
Her Majesty The Queen opening Carsington Water, Derbyshire, May 1992

Above: Wedding of our daughter Emma and Tobias Tennant, 3 September 1963

Below: Greeting guests for Peregrine's 21st birthday celebrations, 19th June 1965

Peregrine, Lord Hartington's 21st birthday celebrations, June 1965

Above: Peregrine's wedding to Amanda Heywood-Lonsdale in the presence of Her Majesty The Queen and Her Majesty The Queen Mother, 28th June 1967

Below: At the dance after the wedding, June 1967. Cecil Beaton, my sisters Nancy Mitford, Pamela Jackson, Diana Mosley, Andrew and myself

With Sophia & Peregrine at Bolton Hall, August 1977

Chatsworth Christmas party, 1965, for children of employees and Pilsley Primary School

On the terrace at Bolton Hall

Collecting

Andrew's passionate interest in adding to the existing art collection began in 1946 when he bought works by Gwen John. However, it was not until the better financial position in the early 1970s that he collected in earnest.

The Devonshire collection had hardly been added to since the 1870s. Most of the paintings and drawings Andrew acquired are of the late 19th or 20th centuries by British artists, including Walter Sickert, William Nicholson, Duncan Grant and L.S. Lowry.

As it was never possible to show all the Devonshire treasures at Chatsworth, Andrew was a generous lender to exhibitions all over the world.

He also enjoyed the company of artists. Long friendships with the painter Lucian Freud and the sculptress Angela Conner resulted in the acquisition of many examples of their work, often involving the commissioning of portraits of family and friends.

Andrew liked to encourage artists at the start of their careers, and when he was in his eighties he delighted in purchasing works from Derbyshire artists Gordon Liddle, Duncan Wood and sculptor Tom Freeston.

Viewing the parure display at the opening of the 'Treasures from Chatsworth' exhibition at the Royal Academy of Arts, 1980

In 1994 Andrew and his Trustees bought the portrait of Georgiana, Duchess of Devonshire by Thomas Gainsborough. This painting had led a chequered career and we were all delighted when it came to Chatsworth

The fan of a RB211-524-H
jet engine made by apprentices
at Rolls-Royce in Derby and
presented to Andrew in 1998

'White Tulips'
by William Nicholson

It was at Mrs Ian Fleming's house that Andrew and I met the young artist Lucian Freud. The two men shared an interest in horseracing, and enjoyed each other's company. Lucian was one of our first guests at Chatsworth in 1959, when he began a giant mural of cyclamen in a bathroom.

An early patron, Andrew bought the painting of his sister Elizabeth in 1950. More than half a century of acquisitions followed, resulting in a series of family portraits and other works. Freud painted six members of the Cavendish family, spanning three generations, over twenty-two years.

Andrew also bought early Freud drawings and a rare linocut of a racehorse. At his request 'Large Interior, W.9.' was purchased by the Chatsworth Settlement Trustees in 1974.

The six family portraits by Lucian Freud are a unique group, and the two peaceful Samuel Palmer watercolours are examples of their time which even Chatsworth lacked. His many purchases were simply his choice. Among the best must be William Nicholson's 'White Tulips'.

The Sabine bathroom at Chatsworth

'Portrait of a Man', 1971-72

(11th Duke of Devonshire) by Lucian Freud

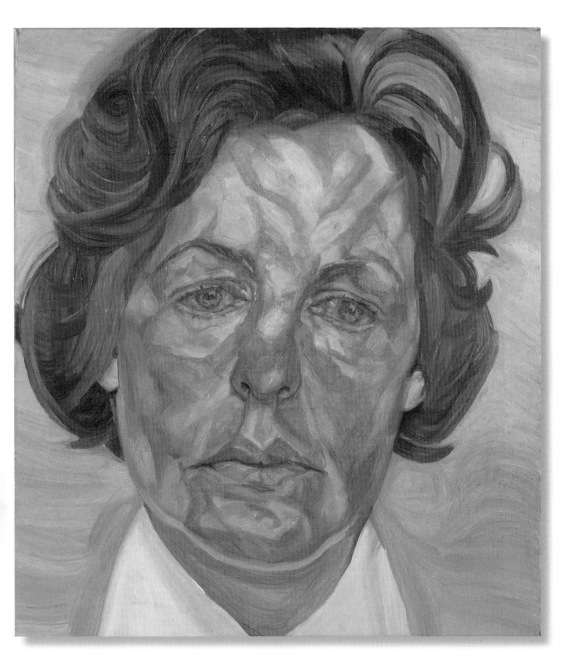

'Woman in a White Shirt', 1958-60

(The Duchess of Devonshire) by Lucian Freud

Andrew in his book-lined sitting room at Chatsworth

At home his chief interests were books, pictures, sculpture and minerals – and the garden. Books were a habit, a lifelong addiction. Until his sight began to fail I never saw him without a book in his hand. At Chatsworth the Lower Library was his sitting room and he filled the shelves with his admired authors. A collection of first editions of Winston Churchill's works pleased him greatly. A shelf was devoted to disasters. Volumes gathered together over the years were a perfect background for the classical library furniture and quirky objects of unknown origin but very dear to their owner.

Towards the end of his life he started to build up a comprehensive Irish library. Every Christmas he enjoyed restocking guest bedrooms, providing each with a wide-ranging miniature library for bedtime enjoyment.

In the Library at Chatsworth with Bracken and Nobby

He bought at auction rare illustrated botanical books by Curtis, Ehret, Redouté, Sibthorp and Trew. Thornton's '*Temple of Flora*' and camellia books were his favourites, reflecting his pride at the annual flowering of the Victoria Regia lily and many species of camellia in the Chatsworth greenhouses. I am told he had the best collection in private hands of these exquisite publications.

A selection of his favourite books from Andrew's bedroom

Andrew became the major shareholder in Heywood Hill, the bookshop in Curzon Street, London, where my sister Nancy had worked as a shop assistant during the war. For ten years he gave an annual money prize for "a lifetime's contribution to the enjoyment of books". All the Derbyshire Mayors and their consorts were invited to the presentation party at Chatsworth, so were the estate heads of departments as well as literary friends and customers of the bookshop. They sometimes made strange table-fellows, but with a jazz band playing that was part of the fun.

Tom Stoppard presenting the Heywood Hill Prize 1995 to Patrick O'Brien,
with John Saumarez Smith, one of the prize judges, and Andrew

In 2002 JK Rowling presented the Heywood Hill Prize to Michael Frayn.
Pictured here with prize judges Sir Michael Howard, Jane Gardam and Andrew

In the Lower Library at Chatsworth

Andrew's minerals on the floor of the west hall at Chatsworth

From 1959 Andrew pursued the family interest in collecting minerals established by Duchess Georgiana and her son, the 6th Duke, nearly two hundred years earlier. He acquired specimens both locally and worldwide and displayed them around the house.

Gardening

Andrew inherited his father's enthusiasm for gardening, especially his interest in spring- and autumn-flowering bulbs. He planted thousands of species crocuses himself, most notably around the weeping ash at the entrance to the house. He preferred these little flowers to schemes on a grand scale.

He worked with three long-serving head gardeners to improve the Chatsworth specialities of prize-winning camellias and grapes. The Display Greenhouse he had built in 1970 provides three climates for a variety of fruit and flowers rarely seen in Derbyshire. Between us we created many striking features in the garden, including the Serpentine Hedge (1953), the Maze (1962) and the re-vitalised Kitchen Garden (1991-93), as well as adding the first important sculpture for 150 years ('War Horse, 1991' by Dame Elisabeth Frink). All the Grade 1 garden buildings, including the Cascade, its house and Flora's Temple, were virtually re-built. In 1999, at Andrew's suggestion, Angela Conner created her water sculpture 'Revelation'.

Gardening in the softer climate of southern Ireland meant more tender species could be grown at Lismore Castle (the family home in Co Waterford), particularly magnolias, camellias and rhododendrons.

The Display Greenhouse at Chatsworth, constructed in 1970

Inspecting lemons in the greenhouse at Chatsworth

With former Chatsworth head gardener, Denis Hopkins, in the orchid house. Denis, Bert Link and Jim Link were head gardeners who each worked at Chatsworth for 50 years – a unique record which can never be achieved now

'Revelation'
by Angela Conner, 1999

Andrew in the tropical section of the Display Greenhouse

In front of the weeping ash on the north drive, surrounded by the spring bulbs he planted

At Compton Place, Eastbourne, c. 1995

On the west drive at Chatsworth

Racing

Andrew's first and lasting sporting passion was racing. As a schoolboy he risked the sack from Eton by regularly going to Windsor races and acting as the school bookmaker. Cambridge was conveniently near to Newmarket and he took full advantage of it.

The early years of his partnership with his friend and trainer Bernard van Cutsem were reasonably successful, but his dreams were realised in the filly 'Park Top', a bargain buy at 500 guineas. She won many races; the most important being the King George & Queen Elizabeth Stakes at Ascot in 1969, and was subsequently second in the Prix de l'Arc de Triomphe. He wrote a book about her, '*A Romance of the Turf*', which reveals as much about the author as it does about the mare.

Left: 'Park Top' with Maureen Foley, her groom throughout her career

Below: After 'Park Top' won the Prix Foy at Longchamps, 7 September 1969, with her jockey Lester Piggott and trainer Bernard van Cutsem

King George VI & Queen Elizabeth
Stakes, Ascot, 26 July 1969

'Park Top' winning
in Paris and at Ascot

Prix d'Hédouville, Longchamps, 8 September 1968

Andrew owned two good National Hunt horses, 'The Dunce' and 'Gay George', trained by Fulke Walwyn. They won 18 races between them.

'Gay George', named by an innocent Irish farmer

Duck Row in the estate village of Pilsley was the inspiration for the name of this horse

With Sophia at the races

Over 18 years Andrew sent 39 horses to be trained by James Toller. 21 were the winners of 58 races. Their biggest win was 'Compton Place' in the 1997 July Cup and two weeks after his owner's death, 'Bachelor Duke' won the Irish 2000 Guineas, a "classic" race. He carried Sophia's colours.

Other Sporting Interests

Fishing was another great love of Andrew's. His uncle, Charlie Cavendish, married Adele Astaire (Fred's sister) in 1932. Charlie was given Lismore Castle in Co. Waterford by his father, the 9th Duke of Devonshire, as a wedding present. Sadly he was a victim of alcoholism and died at Lismore in March 1944 aged 39. He left that magical place to Andrew, who at that time had no prospect of being his father's heir.

We both loved Lismore and Ireland and spent the month of April there for over fifty years. Andrew also went there for the first fortnight of February, the salmon fishing season opening on the 1st of that month.

There were some anxious years when the activities of the IRA were at their unpredictable height. The Irish government insisted on police protection for Andrew, as an obvious target for kidnap, and up to fourteen Garda looked after him when at Lismore or Careysville, the fishing lodge. Mercifully that is all in the past, forgotten as a bad dream. It did not affect his love for Ireland and the Irish, which remained with him all his life.

With his ghillie Paddy Egan after catching a 28lb salmon, 1975

In the fishing hut at Careysville, 1997

Peregrine and Emma with their first salmon, Careysville, 1961.
(A composite photograph from the family album)

On a boat
trip down the
Blackwater to
the estuary,
c. 1970

Andrew fishing for salmon on the river Blackwater, 1986

At Careysville, Co. Cork, 1986

Andrew said he was "rotten" at school games and he never enjoyed shooting, but he loved fox hunting.

At a meet of the Quorn Hounds

Left: The Lyke Wake Walk – John Oaksey, Brough Scott & Rupert Lycett Green amongst the party
Right: At 15,000 feet in Peru, 1971

He enjoyed walking tours in Peru, the Pyrénées and Greece with Patrick Leigh Fermor and friends. In 1978 he completed the Lyke Wake Walk, 39 miles across the North Yorkshire Moors.

Andrew believed strongly in public access to privately owned moorland and was ahead of his time in making thousands of acres across his Derbyshire and Yorkshire moors available to walkers nearly forty years ago.

On the moor above Bolton Abbey,
Yorkshire, 1958

Andrew and his dog Portly in a grouse butt
at Bolton Abbey c. 1958

In the 1950s he became Chairman of the Lawn Tennis Association. He was passionate about golf, watching every hole of The Open on television each year, and was knowledgeable about many sports including bowls, cricket, football and rugby. He was proud to hold honorary posts with numerous sporting clubs, including President of Chesterfield F.C. and of Derbyshire County Cricket Club, and Vice-President of the All England Lawn Tennis Club.

Left: At the bowling club in Baslow, Derbyshire, May 1995

Below: With Tony Benn MP at the reception for Chesterfield Football Club's achievements in the FA Cup 1996/97

Entertaining

Andrew's reputation as a generous and imaginative host reached its zenith in the 1990s. In 1991 we invited all the Golden Wedding couples in Derbyshire to mark our own anniversary – 3,700 people had tea in a huge marquee covering the South Lawn and the Sea Horse Fountain. Ten years later a smaller number reconvened to celebrate our Diamond Weddings with a "wartime" tea party.

For the Tercentenary of the dukedom in 1994 Andrew commissioned a pageant enacting the history of the Cavendish family. 6,000 people enjoyed two riverside performances. On the second night a large sum was raised for The Children's Society.

For his fiftieth anniversary as duke he gave a dinner party for 2,000 people to which he invited all on the Chatsworth estate and many who had shared his years in public life.

With our grandson William Burlington at the celebrations for his 21st birthday, 1990

The Inner Court tented over and a dance floor laid for William's birthday party, 1990

The South Lawn and the statue of Endymion tented over for the dinner for William's coming of age, 1990

The stage and tiered seating on the riverside for the Tercentenary celebrations, 1994.
Andrew planted an oak tree to mark the site in the park

May 12th 1994,
celebrations for the
Tercentenary of the
dukedom

Tea for 3,700 for the golden wedding
celebration on 19th April 1991

The diamond wedding couple, September 2001

At the fancy dress party to mark his fiftieth
year as duke and our 80th birthdays, July 2000.
I wore the dress made by Worth for Louise,
wife of the 8th Duke of Devonshire, for the
famous Devonshire House Ball of 1897

Inside the marquee on the South Lawn for the
party in July 2000. A fence surrounds the
Sea Horse Fountain

In his autobiography Andrew deals frankly with the subject of alcoholism, a curse which has afflicted many members of his family, including his father and his uncle Charlie. The damage it causes not only to the sufferer but to all those around, especially the children, is impossible to imagine unless you have seen it at close quarters – and it seems that most people have. With a huge effort of will he managed to win the battle and, in spite of depression, near-blindness and general malaise, he remained a teetotaller for the last twenty years of his life.

Andrew, 2001

Andrew, 1995

Andrew's Legacy

From the mid 1970s, with the death duties paid, Andrew turned his attention to expanding and improving the provisions for visitors to Chatsworth. These sprung from the wish to inform new generations of the importance of the land and how it is managed. The commercial interests of increasing income for the upkeep of Chatsworth, its garden and park were addressed. The pioneering educational children's farmyard opened in 1973, followed by the farm shop in 1977.

But still the future security of Chatsworth was not guaranteed. Andrew and our son decided on a longer-term, almost unprecedented solution. In 1981, after three years of negotiations with the government, Chatsworth was leased for 99 years to a charitable foundation, the Chatsworth House Trust. Its object being "to ensure the preservation of the house, its essential contents, garden and park for the public benefit". The House Trust was funded by a large endowment from the family, including proceeds of sales from the private art collection.

Entrance ticket sales plus 10% of the turnover from the house shops and restaurant, together with endowment income, covered the Trust's full operating costs for the first time in 2004. The family is represented on the House Trust's Council and pays a market rent for the rooms they occupy.

Chatsworth from the Canal

On the west drive, 1999

The 1980s was a cheerful period of consolidation and expansion at all the family estates. New businesses were created from existing estate resources and a massive programme of restoration work, both inside and out of doors, was embarked upon at Chatsworth.

The 1990s was the decade for anniversaries and celebrations of long-standing achievements, while Andrew continued to undertake a full diary of public duties with enthusiasm.

The pinnacle was reached for Andrew in 1996 when Her Majesty The Queen invested him a Knight of the Garter.

Andrew with our son and grandson

At the entrance of St George's Chapel, Windsor Castle, after his investiture as a
Knight of the Garter, June 1996

Sheffield & District Orchid Society's annual show at Edensor

At a dinner for the Centre for the Study of Jewish-Christian Relations

The private tragedy of the last two decades of his life was loss of eyesight. Years before it usually strikes he was afflicted by senile macular dystrophy. It took its course and he was practically blind for the last two or three years. It was so sad to think he still bought books but could not read them.

I never once heard him complain about it. Only his intimates realised how badly it affected him and how it added to the depression from which he suffered.

He struggled on as best he could with the public duties which had made him so well-known and so much loved and admired. The number of charities and other organisations for which he worked seemed endless. It was the generosity of spirit, the time and interest he gave which counted wherever he went. The total lack of pomposity, his brilliant way of making people laugh endeared him to everyone he met.

Visiting Eastbourne, 2003

Above: Opening the new adventure playground with our grandchildren, Declan and Nancy Morrison, March 1998

Below: Christmas Day 1999 with some of our children, grandchildren and great-grandchildren in the west hall

With the arrival of great-grandchildren, our family extended to four generations. The Chatsworth estate continued its tradition of long service. By 2007 there had been 237 awards for 25 years service and 117 for 40 years.

Having survived the uncertainties of the 1950s and taxation, Andrew ensured that Chatsworth is now better cared for and more used than ever before. Jobs have been created or retained in many specialist fields and over 550 people are now employed on the Derbyshire estate.

John Pearson wrote in *Stags & Serpents*, 2002: "by making such an extraordinary success from the near disaster they inherited…, they have also laid down new foundations which provide Chatsworth's best hope of survival."

The staff at Chatsworth assembled on the south front, 1997

Right:
Meeting the press to mark the one-millionth visitor to the Chatsworth farmyard, autumn 2003

Below:
Greeting the five-millionth visitor to Chatsworth, 16th October 1998

Above: With Ian Gregory of The Polite Society, of which Andrew was Patron-in-Chief

Below Left: Our house in Chesterfield Street, Mayfair

Below Right: Andrew was Proprietor and Chairman of Pratt's Club, St James's, London

In his sitting room at Chatsworth

Andrew died at home on 3rd May 2004. The day of his funeral was sunny and the park looked extraordinarily beautiful in new green. A huge crowd turned out, many of whom were not born when he found himself in charge of Chatsworth and so much more.

He was the first to say how lucky he was throughout his life, and the fun and enjoyment he had and gave to others was legendary. As his wife, I saw all that underlined a thousand times. Like everyone, he could be difficult, but like very few, he was never boring.

10th May 2004 – The cortège left Chatsworth for the service and burial at St Peter's Church, Edensor. Members of staff lined the route and over 3,000 people paid their respects

Hundreds more came to the memorial services at Bolton Abbey, in London and at Lismore in Ireland. I received over 3,000 letters, cards and messages.

To quote from a few – "Andrew was a man of great determination and courage... often one step ahead... buying works of art or in his comments on politics...

His enthusiasm for life, his generosity, courtesy, thoughtfulness…, charm, lack of affectation, self-deprecation, independence of spirit and sense of fun were a heartening inspiration.

He represented a more noble and dutiful age. With his modesty, bravery and mild eccentricity, he was everything a duke should be."

Andrew Robert Buxton Cavendish, Duke of Devonshire, K.G., P.C., M.C., 1920 – 2004